First World War
and Army of Occupation
War Diary
France, Belgium and Germany

38 DIVISION
115 Infantry Brigade,
Brigade Trench Mortar Battery
1 July 1916 - 29 August 1916

WO95/2562/4

The Naval & Military Press Ltd
www.nmarchive.com
Published in association with The National Archives

Published by

The Naval & Military Press Ltd

Unit 10 Ridgewood Industrial Park,

Uckfield, East Sussex,

TN22 5QE England

Tel: +44 (0) 1825 749494

www.naval-military-press.com

www.nmarchive.com

This diary has been reprinted in facsimile from the original. Any imperfections are inevitably reproduced and the quality may fall short of modern type and cartographic standards.

© **Crown Copyright**
Images reproduced by permission of The National Archives, London, England, 2015.

Contents

Document type	Place/Title	Date From	Date To
Heading	38th Division 115th Infy Bde Trench Mortar Bty Jly-Aug 1916		
Heading	115th Inf. Bde. 38th Div. War Diary 115th Trench Mortar Battery. July 1916		
War Diary	Toutencourt	01/07/1916	01/07/1916
War Diary	Acheux	02/07/1916	03/07/1916
War Diary	Buire Sur Ancre	04/07/1916	04/07/1916
War Diary	Mametz	05/07/1916	12/07/1916
War Diary	Warloy-Baillon	13/07/1916	13/07/1916
War Diary	Couin	13/07/1916	14/07/1916
War Diary	Coigneux.	15/07/1916	18/07/1916
War Diary	Colincamps	20/07/1916	28/07/1916
War Diary	Bus Les Artois	29/07/1916	29/07/1916
War Diary	Chandas	30/07/1916	30/07/1916
War Diary	St. Omer	31/07/1916	31/07/1916
War Diary	Wulverdinghe	31/07/1916	01/08/1916
War Diary	Merckeghem	03/08/1916	19/08/1916
War Diary	Poperinghe	19/08/1916	19/08/1916
War Diary	Ypres	19/08/1916	19/08/1916
War Diary	Wieltje Farm Turco Farm Sector	20/08/1916	29/08/1916
Map	115th Trench Mortar Battery Appendix I		
Diagram etc	115th Trench Mortar Battery Appendix II		

38TH DIVISION
115TH INFY BDE

TRENCH MORTAR BTY

JLY-AUG 1916

115th Inf.Bde.
38th Div.

WAR DIARY

115th TRENCH MORTAR BATTERY.

J U L Y & Aug

1 9 1 6

Army Form C. 2118

WAR DIARY
or
INTELLIGENCE SUMMARY.
(Erase heading not required.)

11 S Trench Mortar Battery July 1916   Vol 4

Place	Date	Hour	Summary of Events and Information	Remarks and references to Appendices
TOUTENCOURT	1/7/16	4/30 pm	Left billets at TOUTENCOURT for ACHEUX. Instructions for action between SOMME & ANCRE received.	
ACHEUX	2/7/16	10 am	Bivouac in Wood E. of ACHEUX will remainder of Bde.	
	3/7/16	4 pm	Left ACHEUX for BUIRE SUR ANCRE. On this, as on all other long marches recently the training area, the advantage of moving by night were apparent, the men looking much less tiring.	
BUIRE SUR ANCRE	4/7/16	2 am	Billeted in BUIRE with remainder of the Bde. During the afternoon the O.C. visited HQ 7th Division near FRICOURT	
MAMETZ	5/7/16	4/30 pm	Left BUIRE 1/30 p.m. and bivouaced on MAMETZ - BRAY road, S.W. of MAMETZ, & near remainder of Bde. O.C. 39/st. Mortar reported Bn route to CATERPILLAR TRENCH	
	6/7/16		CATERPILLAR TRENCH & Sopha Annum Dumps reconnoitred during morning. On subsequent events O.C. reported as follows on 9/7/16 " In accordance with operation Order No. 62 at 8/30 a.m. on 7th inst. 11 S L TM B occupied positions made WEST & RY of CATERPILLAR WOOD. At 8 a.m. an intense bombardment was opened, 4 of the southern end of the EAST side of MAMETZ WOOD, for being strong the particularly	
	7/7/16		about point A (ref. Sketch map of MAMETZ WOOD received 4/7/16) where a M.G. had previously been erected, and through these the assaulting Infantry (11 Bde) advanced. Between 8/30 & 10 a.m. as the Infantry advanced	

WAR DIARY or INTELLIGENCE SUMMARY

Army Form C. 2118.

11 S Trench Mortar Battery July 1916

Place	Date	Hour	Summary of Events and Information	Remarks and references to Appendices
MAMETZ	7/7/16		Two hostile MGs were located & in conjunction with a Lewis gun & the 11 S. Bde., were engaged. Costly Stokes bombs burst the nearer of the hostile MGs in order to even momentarily divert the most murderous continually increasing enemy Lewis gun fire. MGs were not again brought into action within range of the Stokes guns & from close observation it is conclusive that both hostile M.G.s were destroyed. Heavy casualties inflicted on the enemy. A third MG was located but it was out of range of the Stokes guns. It was suggested by the Lewis gun, but this did not seem to have any effect on it. I desire to place on record my appreciation of the unflagging energy & determination in the part of Lieut. A Jeffreys & 2/Lts. W. O. Jones in keeping the guns supplied with ammunition in spite of the enormous difficulties encountered. In all some 450 rounds were used. Some carried up by the sections commanded by these Officers with the exception of 90 rounds carried by a fatigue party of the 17th R.W.F." The supply of sufficient ammunition was a matter of very great difficulty, and was owing to the ground on account of the heavy rain made matters very much worse that a carrying parties other than those of my command found great difficulty in moving about & so that a fatigue party of 100 men of the 17th R.W.F. who were intended to supplement the carrying up of ammunition	

WAR DIARY
or
INTELLIGENCE SUMMARY.
(Erase heading not required.)

Army Form C. 2118.

115 Trench Mortar Battery   July 1916

Place	Date	Hour	Summary of Events and Information	Remarks and references to Appendices
MAMETZ	7/7/16		Fired a destructive bombardment to keep 2 S.A.A. guns adequately supplied with ammunition. Careful organization is essential. Casualties: 1 man wounded-shot still	
	8/7/16		The ammunition party returned to Bivouac at 10 a.m. At 2 noon orders to officer the Bn. was received today, but notice = necessary sent by Lieut. A. Ralph in ordering bivouac at 10/7/15 a.m. was received. Lieut. Kittred, in CATERPILLAR WOOD died of wounds this day. Lieut. His party began to receive bivouac at 8 p.m.	
	10/7/16		The battery stood to at 3 p.m. when the bombardment preceding the attack of the 113 & 114 Bdes on MAMETZ WOOD opened. Subsequent events were reported in hour of Ralph's report. At 11 p.m. 10/7/16 Batt. moved to MAMETZ WOOD with 1 gun shown in accordance with 115 Bde. Operation Order No. 64. The gun was in action shortly after 3 a.m.	
	11/7/16		at the point where QUADRANGLE SUPPORT trench enters the WOOD, from which position it could have dealt effectively with any attempt to enter the WOOD by means of that trench. Nothing of importance occurred during the day. Three of my men with a duty orderly on duty at the gun did work in recovering several badly wounded men who had hitherto been overlooked. They also cleared up a large dug-out near the gun position, which was afterwards used as Bde HQ.	

WAR DIARY 115 Trench Mortar Battery
INTELLIGENCE SUMMARY.
(Erase heading not required.)

Army Form C. 2118.

July 1916

Instructions regarding War Diaries and Intelligence Summaries are contained in F.S. Regs., Part II. and the Staff Manual respectively. Title pages will be prepared in manuscript.

Place	Date	Hour	Summary of Events and Information	Remarks and references to Appendices
MAMETZ	1/7/16		by the relieving Bde. At dusk the gun was withdrawn from its somewhat exposed position & held in readiness, near Bde HQ., to proceed to any part of "WOOD." at 6 a.m. on the 12th. Guns relieved by the "62nd T.M.B."	
	1/7/16		Although heavily shelled throughout the night, our casualties were only 2 men wounded. The battery, under orders from Bde.H.Q. were ready to move off to entrain at Buire-time from 2 p.m., but at 8 p.m. information was received that the movement was postponed to 4/30 a.m. 13/7/16.	
WARLOY- BAILLON	13/7/16		and the remainder of the Bde., the battery left Buire near MAMETZ at 5 a.m. and after a march which tried the men more than on account of the heavy demands recently made of them by the extreme of the 7th & 11th, arrived at billets at WARLOY-BAILLON at 2 p.m., remaining in readiness to move again in further an.	
COUIN	15/7/16		The Battery with remainder of Bde., left Warloy at COUIN at 8/20 p.m., arriving at 10/30 p.m. Before into bivouac.	
	14/7/16		Arrangements made to relieve 144 T.M.B. trenches. Infantry relief today.	
COIGNEUX	15/7/16		Took over from 144 T.M.B. trenches near COIGNEUX, Bde H.Q. being 3-4 miles distant. 144 T.M.B's only armament is live or special occasion, but as no proper	

14

WAR DIARY 115 Trench Mortar Battery

Army Form C. 2118.

INTELLIGENCE SUMMARY.

(Erase heading not required.)

Instructions regarding War Diaries and Intelligence Summaries are contained in F.S. Regs., Part II. and the Staff Manual respectively. Title pages will be prepared in manuscript.

July 1916

Place	Date	Hour	Summary of Events and Information	Remarks and references to Appendices
COIGNEUX	15/7/16		Building emplacements & then holding the line it was necessary to wait for lidelite in COLINCAMPS.	
	16/7/16		C.O. visited O.C. Right Section. with view to Stokes guns cooperating in mending parise, but own assistance is not required.	
	17/7/16		Rde front line reconnoitred to select positions H.P. for emplacements	
COLINCAMPS	20/7/16		Battery Hd: COIGNEUX at 5 p.m. Moved into billets at COLIN CAMPS at 8 p.m. Rde moved on to the R.E. assistance has been reserved for building emplacements.	
	21/7/16		Line reconnoitred with view to sabotage of Stokes trench left in divine exp by 146 Rde. This week, however, being given to the relief by Salvage squads. Practised for demonstration of Mountain raid in conjunction with Stokes Guns, organised by 11th K.S.W.B. Employees meant definitely estion the line by R.E. Officer i/c of Brigade	
	22/7/16		Another practice for demonstration took place on 6 emplacements. Owing to knowledge of line this week, offer impossible by day, is very difficult at night.	
	23/7/16		Practice for demonstration turned on emplacements continues	
	24/7/16		Demonstration of Mountain raid in conjunction with Stokes guns by 11th K.O.C. B & H (ibid) Personage of F.O.C. 115 Brig. Our shooting was excellent.	

WAR DIARY or INTELLIGENCE SUMMARY

Army Form C. 2118.

115 Trench Mortar Battery July 1916

(Erase heading not required.)

Instructions regarding War Diaries and Intelligence Summaries are contained in F. S. Regs., Part II. and the Staff Manual respectively. Title pages will be prepared in manuscript.

Place	Date	Hour	Summary of Events and Information	Remarks and references to Appendices
COLINCAMPS	25/7/16		At 8 p.m. O.C. 115th S.M.B. accompanying retaliation for enemy minenwerfers, came to decide Officer 2/Lt. J. Rhonie with 2 gun teams went into the line. Dug-outs were very inconvenient. Besides disorganising & weakening the working parties, whose work on the new emplacements had been continuous & most urgent, reconnaissance was impossible & new emplacements inevitable. One gun placed in a position indicated by a company commander had to be withdrawn at daybreak, the position being untenable by day.	
	26/7/16		8 S.R. minnin fired. After the enemy had put up a stubborn resistance, we established our supremacy as far as trench mortars are concerned. Work on emplacements continued.	
	27/7/16		As regards trench mortars, the line was much quieter; we only found it necessary to fire 4 rounds in retaliation at the rate of 6 rounds for 1 of the enemy's. Lieut. Ralph G. Cann relieved 2/Lt. J. Rhonie this month. Work on emplacements continued.	
	28/7/16		Relief, in bullets & lime, of Eng 60 att. T.M.B. completed by 7 p.m. It was observed that the 60th T.M.B. did not keep their guns in the temporary emplacements in	lu

WAR DIARY or INTELLIGENCE SUMMARY

Army Form C. 2118.

115th Trench Mortar Battery July 1916

Place	Date	Hour	Summary of Events and Information	Remarks and references to Appendices
COLINCAMPS	23/7/16		Offr. sent his team back at their own request H.Q. to be sent into action when required. Through holidaymakers, this eruption does not seem so satisfactory as own. Any other new can open fire at a moment's notice. The emplacements we started should be ready in two or three days.	
BUS LES ARTOIS	29/7/16		Left COLINCAMPS for BUS LES ARTOIS at noon. Arrived at 1/45 p.m., marching with M.G. Coy. remainder of Bde carrying out our own programme. The infantry were not relieved up until this morning.	
CHANDAS	30/7/16		Right section left BUS at 4/15 a.m. Arrived with 10th S.W.B. and 1 section M.G. Coy to CHANDAS which was reached at 4/50 p.m. This section left for ST. OMER by train at 7/51 p.m. Handcarts were unloaded, trailers being packed under animal wagon, the carts themselves, wheels uppermost, was used as timbers. Left section left BUS at 5/30 a.m. with 11th S.W.B. & section M.G. Coy. reached CHANDAS at 12/15 p.m. Then 8 handcarts, loaded, were loaded on 1/2 a truck. They left for ST. OMER at 11/51 p.m.	
ST. OMER	31/7/16		Right section arrived at 1/56 a.m., left section at 5 a.m.	
WULVERDINGHE	31/7/16		Marching from ST. OMER, and receiving horses from the infantry at WATTEN,	

Army Form C. 2118.

WAR DIARY
or
INTELLIGENCE SUMMARY.

115 Trench Mortar Battery

July 1916

(Erase heading not required.)

Instructions regarding War Diaries and Intelligence Summaries are contained in F. S. Regs., Part II. and the Staff Manual respectively. Title pages will be prepared in manuscript.

Place	Date	Hour	Summary of Events and Information	Remarks and references to Appendices
WULVERDINGHE	24/7/16		Right section reached its billets in WULVERDINGHE at 8am, while the Left section arrived at 12 noon. The men were extremely tired after the marching yesterday & today and the railway journey, and rested most of the day. By the kindness of O.o.C. 10th. & 11th. S.W.B. our men were given hot tea en route by the cooks of those units, to whom our rations of tea on such a sudden hour were handed over.
			Signed	
			[signature]	
			Lieut.	
			Officer Commanding	
			115th. Trench Mortar Battery	

Army Form C. 2118.

WAR DIARY
or
INTELLIGENCE SUMMARY.
(Erase heading not required.)

115th Trench Mortar Battery
August (1)

Vol 5

Instructions regarding War Diaries and Intelligence Summaries are contained in F.S. Regs., Part II. and the Staff Manual respectively. Title pages will be prepared in manuscript.

Place	Date	Hour	Summary of Events and Information	Remarks and references to Appendices
WULVERDINGHE	1/8/16		Resting at WULVERDINGHE.	
MERCKEGHEM	2/8/16		Left billets at WULVERDINGHE, which had been occupied since 31/7/16, for MERCKEGHEM (in the BOLLEZEELE area) the Division being in Corps Reserve (VIII Corps). Arrived in new billets 7/15 a.m. Program of training in Physical Training, Rifle & Bayonet exercises, Musketry, Close order Drill, Guard Duties, Route marches, Saluting drill, Bivouac, Village fighting, Organisation & Administration, Transport, Technical Subjects prepared in accordance with B.M. 603 of 31/8/16, and with commenced	
	4/8/16		Training in above subject commenced. Also course of instruction for 1 Officer, 1 Sergeant, 3 corporals & 3 Privates commenced.	
	6/8/16		Church parades until 16th Welsh Kit inspection by C.O. No training.	
	7/8/16		Training on above as commenced.	
	9/8/16	9/30	Inspection by G.O.C. Kit & equipment. Section Officers in agreed drill generally. Following criticisms. Several unsuitable articles of kit clothing; All men deficient of in coats; men steady on parade, handled arms well; suggested been Officers to join "spirit de tache"; more emphasis to be placed on elementary principles of discipline. 1st course of instruction concluded.	

T2134. Wt. W708-776. 500000. 4/15. Sir J. C. & S.

Army Form C. 2118.

WAR DIARY or INTELLIGENCE SUMMARY

(Erase heading not required.)

115th Trench Mortar Battery

August (2)

Place	Date	Hour	Summary of Events and Information	Remarks and references to Appendices
MERCKEGHEM	9/8/16		Second course of instruction commenced	
	13/8/16		Church parade with 164th held. Battn. used. Report received on G.O.C.'s inspection	
	16/8/16		Training continued. Second course of instruction concluded.	
	18/8/16		Billets, latrines, etc, inspected by A.D.M.S. who was completely satisfied. C.O. attended regimental exercise without troops under G.O.C. Training postponed in progress.	
	19/8/16		Orders to be ready to entrain at BOLLEZEELE at 9 a.m. to relieve 124th Brigade at YPRES received at 5/30 a.m. Left Wellis at MERCKEGHEM, in accordance with Extn. orders, at 9 a.m., entrained at BOLLEZEELE 10/30 a.m., detrained at POPERINGHE at 2 p.m., and went into billets in hop factory near station. 3/Lt. J R Morris on advance party, had	
POPERINGHE			Left MERCKEGHEM at 8 a.m., reported to C.O. at 3 p.m. Others proceeded to take over from 124th TMB as we were not involved in going at VLAMERTINGHE on at first ordered. Left POPERINGHE at 10/15 p.m., detrained at ASYLUM, YPRES, and marched to Wieltje	
YPRES			6/12th TMB on the (CANAL BANK). Left section immediately with 5 guns into the line.	
WIELTJE FARM TURCO FARM SECTOR	20/8/16		WIELTJE FARM — TURCO FARM SECTOR. Relief completed at 3/45 a.m. 20/8/16. B guns at C 15 C 7 1 (2 guns), C 15 C 60 35 (2 guns) and ISOLATION POST, C 22 C 20 15 (1 gun). See map, appendix I. Emplacement under construction at	

Army Form C. 2118.

WAR DIARY
INTELLIGENCE SUMMARY.

115th Trench Mortar Battery   August

(Erase heading not required.)

Place	Date	Hour	Summary of Events and Information	Remarks and references to Appendices
WIELTJE FARM –TURCO FARM SECTOR	20/8/16		C 15 c 35 50, N. of TURCO FARM. First 4 guns came MORTELDGE ESTAMINET and on opp. bank, the 5th covers our positions, while the new ones will cover HIGH COMMAND REDOUBT. They are purely defensive positions, and it is impossible to register any of the guns. 12th TMB did not fire while in our sector.	
	21/8/16		115th Inf. Bde. Defence Scheme, relieving 1st Guards Bde. Defence Scheme, received. 3 N.C.Os received instructions in Gas Duties from Divnl. Gas Officer at H.Q. 16 S.W.B. Special order re Gas, to act on Army, Corps & Divnl. Instructions issued. 1 copy to be posted in each dug out on CANAL BANK. GAS ALARM received on CANAL BANK 8/15 p.m. Sprayers took to arms, wearing gas helmets, until 9/15 p.m.	
	22/8/16		Right section relieved Left section in the line at 11/30 p.m. Work commenced in neighbourhood of ALGERIAN COTTAGE (see sketch map, appendices I & II). All the trenches near the guns here were about 1'6" above the level of ATLAS TR, the main communication trench, very wet. The parapets were low and up bullet proof, bearing head & shoulders exposed to view from HIGH COMMAND REDOUBT. The drain was useless, being choked up. Dug outs were in a bad state.	

Army Form C. 2118.

WAR DIARY
or
INTELLIGENCE SUMMARY.

115th Trench Mortar Battery   Month: August   (4)

(Erase heading not required.)

Place	Date	Hour	Summary of Events and Information	Remarks and references to Appendices
WIELTJE FARM — TURCO FARM SECTOR	22/8/16		First of all three trenches worked on the week. (See Appendix I), were cleaned or pumped out and drainage permitted of the parapet raised by night. The improvement of the H.Q. dugout was also commenced.	
	25/8/16		Left section relieved right section in the line at 11/30 p.m.	
	26/8/16		The clearing of the drain commenced, as well as interlacing with the other work. Our men having to provide an R.E. fatigue party of 1 ofr. 9.10 men, there in addition to the usual ration parties etc., it is now necessary for Officers servants to form the guard on the CANAL BANK at night.	
	28/8/16		2/Lt. FR Morris attended trench mortar demonstration at 2nd Army School of Instruction	
	29/8/16		Left section relieved in the line by right section at 11 p.m.	

B A Wood
Lieut.
O/c 115 T.M. Bat.

Instructions regarding War Diaries and Intelligence Summaries are contained in F. S. Regs., Part II. and the Staff Manual respectively. Title pages will be prepared in manuscript.

WAR DIARY *or* INTELLIGENCE SUMMARY.

(Erase heading not required.)

115th Trench Mortar Battery

Army Form C. 2118.

APPENDIX I

C

August

Place	Date	Hour	Summary of Events and Information	Remarks and references to Appendices
YPRES			Trench map of Brigade area in ST JULIEN SECTOR, SHEET 28 N.W. 2,	

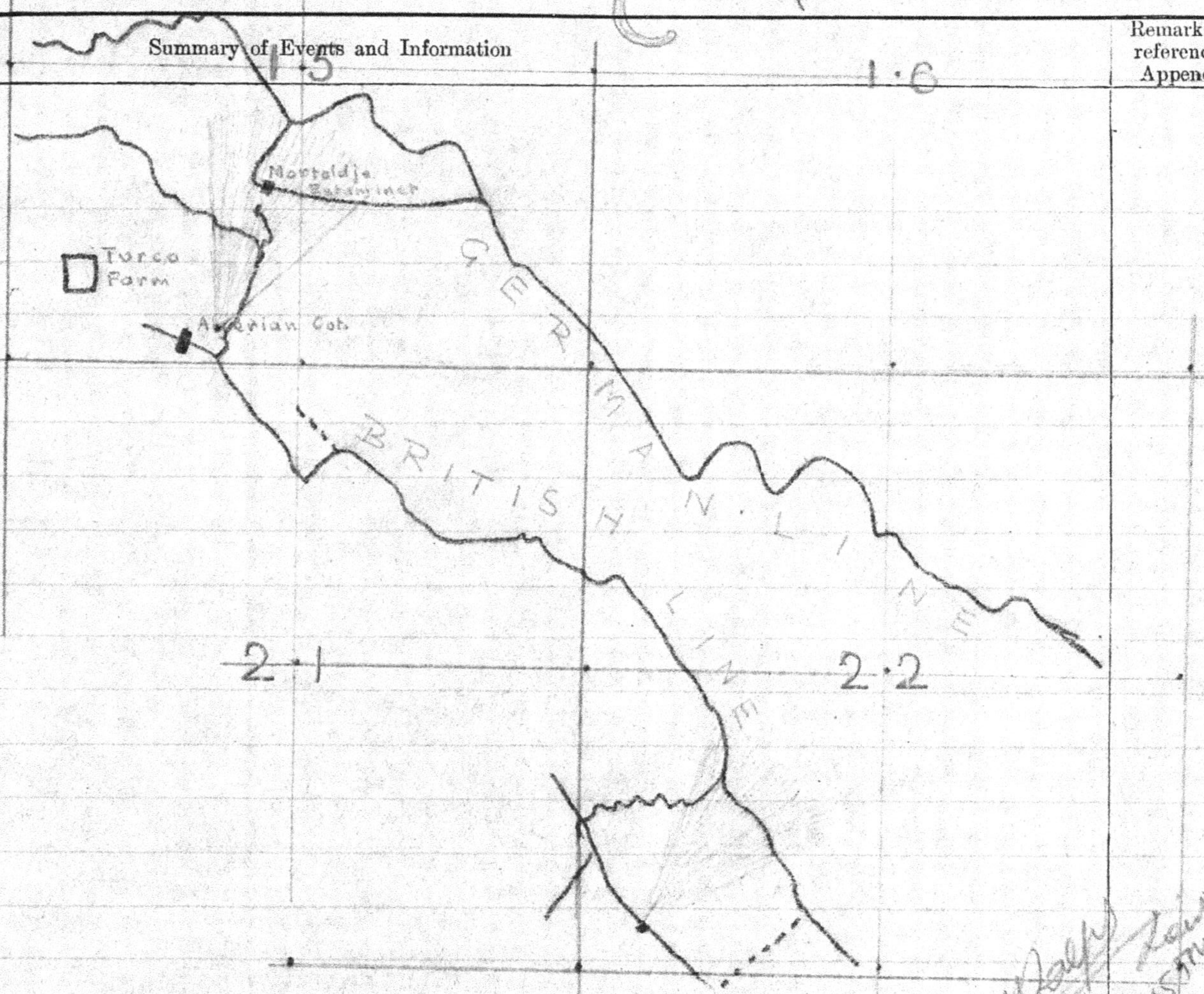

15
1·6
2·1
2·2
Mortaldje Estaminet
Turco Farm
GERMAN LINE
BRITISH LINE

[illegible] Lieut
O.C. 115th T.M.B.

T2134. Wt. W708—776. 500000. 4/15. Sir J. C. & S.

Instructions regarding War Diaries and Intelligence Summaries are contained in F. S. Regs., Part II. and the Staff Manual respectively. Title pages will be prepared in manuscript.

WAR DIARY *or* INTELLIGENCE SUMMARY.

(Erase heading not required.)

115th Trench Mortar Battery

Army Form C. 2118.

APPENDIX II

August

Place	Date	Hour	Summary of Events and Information	Remarks and references to Appendices
YPRES			Sketch map to illustrate positions occupied by guns in ALGERIAN COTTAGE neighborhood. Not to scale	

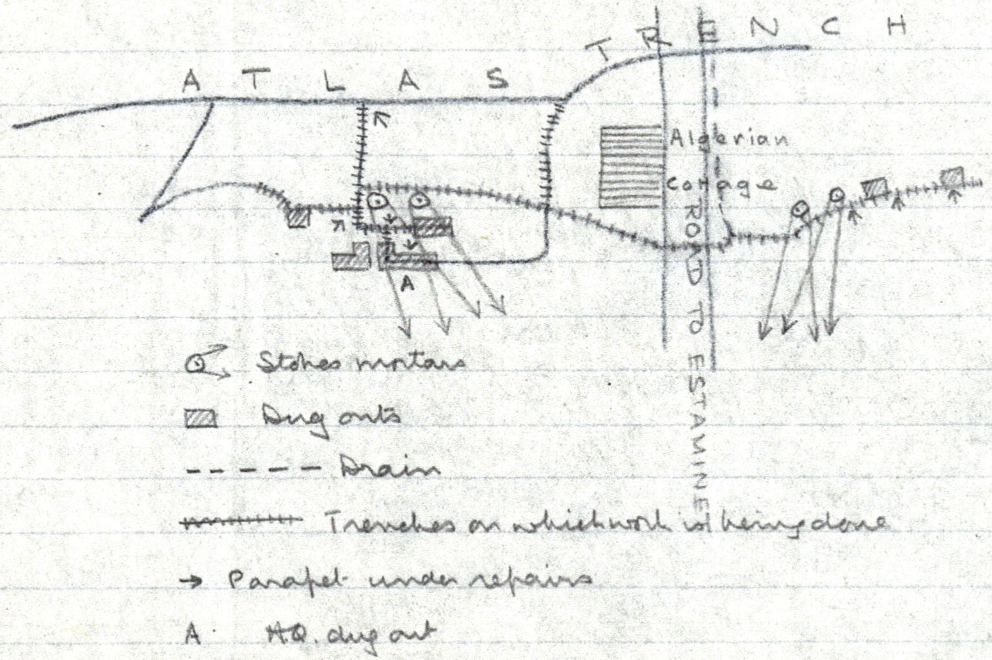

ATLAS TRENCH
Algerian cottage
ROAD TO ESTAMINET
A
Stokes mortars
Dug outs
Drain
Trenches on which work is being done
Parapet under repairs
A H.Q. dug out

www.ingramcontent.com/pod-product-compliance
Lightning Source LLC
Chambersburg PA
CBHW081253170426
43191CB00037B/2137